My Name is Dad

A Father's Story of Loss and Triumph

Contents

Preface

"The imprint of a dad will forever remain on his son."

I remember reading that somewhere. I don't know if I truly left a mark on my son, but I know that the reverse is painfully true for me. The imprint of my son will forever remain on me.

I feel that I must warn you right here, right now. This will not be an easy book to read. It was tough writing it, and it will be tough to read it. Try as I might, there is no easy way to tell a difficult story, and difficult it is.

I must extend a trigger warning to anybody who picks up the book. This is a story about my son's suicide in our home, the days leading up to it, and the aftermath of the tragedy. This book portrays my emotions when I found his body, and my struggle to face every day after that. It will be painful, disturbing, and triggering in every sense, but it might also offer insight into our struggles as we tried to accept the loss, battled through the grief, and found our path to healing.

Though I wouldn't wish for my worst enemy to share this lonely boat with me, if you are in one, I want to extend a hand to you and keep you afloat amidst this raging ocean that threatens to swallow us whole, every day, for the rest of our days. I hope and pray, with every inch of my being, that no father has to live through something as agonizing as watching their own child take his life, but if the story resonates with you, I hope you find peace, closure and acceptance in it. I hope this book helps you make sense of what happened, and stops the loss of a loved one through suicide, taking away everything else in your life.

I might have been through hell, but I have to remind myself that I am still alive. While it is true that my son is gone, I am still here. There are days when I wish for nothing more than to join

1

my son wherever he may be, but that is not an option and I must continue to live my life until it is time to see him again.

Chapter 1: The Day of the Suicide

At exactly 4:30 a.m.., on January 23rd, 2017, my eyes flew open just as they do every day. This has been such a routine to me for so many years, that I have lost count. I have been waking up at 4:30 a.m. and starting my day. I don't even have to try anymore. No matter how late I go to bed, or how tired and exhausted my body has been, I cannot sleep past 4:30 a.m. I do not own an alarm clock. My internal clock is enough to wake me up, on time, without fail, every day.

The room was still dark. The first rays of the sun would soon begin to filter through the curtain, but for now, the faint glow of the lonely streetlight outside was the only source of illumination. My wife was sleeping beside me, and the world was eerily quiet, as it always is during this time of the day. There was nothing out of the ordinary.

January 23rd, 2017. At the moment of my awakening on that day, I had no idea that this date would become etched in my mind. I had no idea that my world was going to turn upside down in a matter of hours. This was just another ordinary day. A Monday, of all days.

The air was still chilly, and I bundled up in a thick robe before heading downstairs for my usual cup of coffee. The thought of a hot, steaming mug of coffee was enough to get me out of bed and hurry downstairs.

I took my time with my coffee, and once I felt energized enough, I walked into my office at 5:00 a.m. to answer all emails, messages, and queries that had accumulated over the weekend. For years, my wife and I have been working from home. We both ran home-based businesses and had set up a nice little corner as our office.

Hours passed as I worked. My wife was up and had woken up my school-going daughter. This too was part of our routine. At 8:30 a.m. every morning, I used to drive my daughter to school.

I got back home after dropping our daughter off, at around 9:00 a.m. I returned to my office to resume work, where my wife was also working. We talked for a bit and then I told her I should go wake our son up.

I had delegated a part of my business to my son, for which I was paying him handsomely. He was a smart kid, and I figured it would be good for him to take on some responsibility of work, while also giving him the necessary exposure, which could prove useful later. He was making very good money for a 21-year-old and was doing pretty great work too.

He had slept long enough today. I went and knocked on his door, but there was silence on the other side. My wife and I always respected my son's privacy. We never opened his door unless he granted us permission to enter. I knocked again to the same lack of response.

Knock-knock-knock-knock.

My wife joined me, as she heard me knocking on his door. She shot me an inquisitive look. He usually answers immediately. She came over and knocked herself, but he didn't respond to either of our knocks. We had been knocking incessantly for quite a while now, and the sound was reverberating throughout the house. It was then that my wife decided to push the door open.

The room was empty. My son was not in his bed.

Bang!

I saw my wife collapse on to the floor. She started wailing loudly, the sound hitting my ears like a hammer. I had no idea what was happening. For some reason, she was convinced that something bad had happened. I tried to console her and get her back up. There was no reason to suspect that anything was amiss.

He might have stepped out for breakfast when we were in the office. He might have gone out to visit his friend in the early morning or he may have spent the night over there. He was an adult after all.

A million explanations for his absence ran through my mind. The one that made sense the most was that he might have stepped out to the garage to exercise where he had a punching bag. He spent a lot of time working out in the garage. I thought, "A little morning exercise never harmed anyone."

So, I walked over to the detached garage and opened the side door.

There he was. I had found him...

But there was no relief at the moment.

He was 4 feet away from me, hanging from the rafters. He was looking at me with eyes that were bloodshot and bulging, his feet dangling in the air. His mouth was hanging open, frozen drool dripping down the side of his mouth. His face was pale, and the veins in his neck bulging and green, like snakes slithering across his neck, constricting him, killing him.

Beneath him, I saw four tires that he must have used to stand on, along with one of our tie-down straps, to hang himself. His cellphone was lying by the side. He set the phone's alarm clock to go off in five-minute intervals. This was probably the alarm he used to wake himself up in the morning.

I did not – could not enter the garage. Though my feet felt heavy, I somehow managed to drag them to the front door of the house, screaming for my wife.

I told her to call 911 immediately.

She grabbed the phone and handed it to me to make the call.

I tried to stop her, but she ran to the garage to see for herself. She showed more self-control at that moment than I had given her credit for previously. She entered the garage without a second thought and pulled me in after her. Together, we lifted his body and tried loosening the strap around his neck, so we could lower him.

His once warm, soft body was stiff against my hands; rigor mortis had already set in. The body was cold and frozen from the cold outside. Judging by the snow on the ground, it looked as if it had been snowing all night.

We hoisted his body and tried to cut the strap he had tightened around his neck. The strap was so tight we actually had to take a knife to it to cut it loose. We finally lowered his lifeless body to the ground.

I noticed that our son had soiled himself; he must have lost control of his bladder even as his soul was leaving his body. There was a stain on the front of his pants, frozen and stiff by now. I wondered how

scared he must have been.

The stench in the garage almost made me gag; the smell of the rubber tires, the stink of urine, and the smell of death combined were overwhelming. It was all around us, all over us, and it would not leave. The stench had settled into the nooks and crannies of the garage, and even though the door of the garage was open, the smell remained.

For the longest time, whenever I walked into the garage, I could smell the same stink again. For the longest time, no matter how much I scrubbed my body and showered, I could feel it lingering on my skin. The tires, the urine. The death.

I don't think anybody who hasn't seen death up close, can understand the certain smell that death exudes. It is ugly, disgusting, and depressing. It seeps into everything; your hair, your skin, your clothes, your house, your car, and your very life.

We lived in that house for 1.5 years after that fateful day. The garage always smelled the same.

We laid our son down on the ground. My wife was shaking him to get him to wake up, and I did not have the heart to stop her. I knew she knew; she knew as well as I that he was dead. But hope is a strange thing, especially hope brought on by grief and desperation.

Panicked, I called 911. The firemen were first on the scene since they were the closest to home. The sheriff then came, and finally, the coroner. The neighbors started peeking out of their windows and doors to see what was going on.

The whole time, my wife lay beside our son on the garage flooring, pleading, screaming, begging him to wake up. Unaware and unconcerned with the rest of our world, she continued shaking his lifeless body.

I eventually pulled her away so the firemen could take a look. They examined his body, checked his heartbeat. The verdict was as we feared; he was indeed dead.

There was nothing anybody could do about it, so the firemen covered him up with a blanket.

Our son was gone. No amount of shaking would ever wake him up.

My wife would not let them cover his face, though. I understood what she meant; once the blanket was placed on his face, he would cease to be a person. He becomes a corpse. There is no coming back from it. Although my wife and I are generally practical, sensible people, and we know, in our hearts, that he is dead, I requested the firemen to oblige by my wife's wishes and leave his face uncovered.

His bulging eyes were looking at me, and I was struggling to decipher what they were trying to say. Were they accusing us? Were they apologizing to us? Were they pleading for help? It felt as if his eyes would bore through my soul forever with these unanswered questions haunting me for the rest of my life.

Looking at him, lying on the ground, I wondered how we managed to hoist him and bring him down from the rafters. Our son was a big boy; he was bulky, muscular, and tall. He was definitely not the kind of young man that a frail man and his wife could handle. But at that moment, we barely felt his weight. All our energy was focused on lowering him to the ground, shaking him awake, with hopes

that the faintest life might still remain in him, or that maybe we were just in time, and, that maybe, we could still save him.

The sheriff and firemen led us inside and sat us down at our own kitchen. They tried talking to us, consoling us, as best they could. They asked questions that my wife and I answered with as much clarity and confidence as we could muster.

"When did you find the body?"

"Was there any drug abuse involved?"

"Had there been a breakup recently?"

"Did he get fired from a job?"

"Was he depressed?"

The questions wouldn't stop; they went on and on for an hour. We told them with as much conviction as we could that there were none of those things involved.

We answered as best as we could, but after a while, I think even the authorities realized that there was no science behind this. There were no signs leading up to it. We did not see this coming. We were as much in the dark about why and how this happened, as the rest of the world.

I've heard of young people committing suicide after a tough breakup with their partners, or when things aren't good at home with the parents, or when they have lost a job or are in a financial crunch.

None of those things were true for our son.

This shocking ordeal made me question myself for a while. Did we not know our son as well as we thought we did? What did we miss? What drove him to this extreme?

Honestly, I don't remember much of that conversation; my mind was still outside, in the garage. Nothing about the next couple of hours was clear; the details of the rest of the day are blurry and hazy, as if I hadn't really lived through it, but observed it from behind a frosted screen.

I saw the coroner taking away the body, wrapped in the blue blanket. They had covered his face after all.

Chapter 2: Deciphering Our Son

Egor.

I try not to take his name too much.

Saying his name still reminds me of how fresh the wounds are.

Anyway, our son was an ordinary kid, by any standards. Of course, year by year, he changed, just like all teenagers and young adults do. We never thought much of it because there were no alarming changes, no acts of rebellion, no fights or arguments at home.

His life outside the home was nothing out of the ordinary either, from what we knew. He had friends, and he had a job. At 16, we had bought him a new car. He would often go and hang out with his friends once he was done with work. In fact, he used to go over to his friend's house almost every other night. Sometimes, he would even spend the weekend over at his friends'.

He had always been a brilliant student and had gotten his bachelor's degree at the age of 16 through the Early Start Program at the university. He was a very organized kid, and when I handed him part of my business to run, he did that with the utmost dedication, always prioritizing work and getting things done. The work from my business that I had delegated to him revolved around helping people with their personal credit, and he made thousands of clients. He was very good with the clients; well-spoken, well-mannered, and always on top of things.

He was a gem.

No, I'm not just saying that because he was my son. This is the general opinion that everyone had about him. He was a hard person to dislike and an absolute pleasure to be around.

We were pretty close-knit family, or so we had always tried to be. We wanted our kids to be comfortable in our company and spend time with us. To spend quality time together, we traveled three to four times a year as the home-based businesses afforded us the luxury of taking a vacation whenever we pleased. So, we would pack up, strap our bags, and go on a road trip across the country. Sometimes to California, sometimes to Arizona. We enjoyed plenty of weekend getaways, and even once took a trip to London as a family.

Everything was okay. Or so it seemed.

Society always expects people who commit suicide to exhibit obvious warning signs or red flags. That was one of the questions we received the most after his death; "Did you see it coming?" "You must have noticed something?" "No?"

As insensitive as that question can be, it also had no response. I was always at a loss for words when anybody asked me that.

I wanted to tell them that that is not always the case. That it is never that simple. That there are often no warning signs before disaster strikes.

There was nothing out of the ordinary with our son. After his death, I tried racking my brain to remember anything that I might have missed before. A call of distress, or a red flag that I did not notice because I was under the illusion that everything was fine with our family.

After much thinking, I could frankly say that the only major difference we noticed over the years was that after he reached the age of 18, he did not want to take family vacations with us anymore. He would make excuses and try to wriggle out of family plans.

He always said that he has business and clients to look after from our home-based business, but it was a pretty glaring fact that he did not want to spend time with mom and dad anymore.

He was 18. Only just becoming a young man. I had been in his shoes once. I understood. He wanted his own freedom; he didn't want to tag along with his parents all the time. That was understandable and nothing too extraordinary. I bet all of us have felt that way when growing up. Anyway, that's how I looked at it and gave him the space he required. We always asked him to come along but did not push him once he had asserted that he would much rather stay at home.

That was it.

His relationship with my wife and I was great. He wasn't quiet or isolated or reserved. He used to talk to us a lot, about any and everything, but he never once mentioned suicide, or that something was wrong or bothering him.

He had become very religious over the years. He would go to church every Sunday and would discuss the Bible with my wife and me. His faith in God was unshakeable.

He was kind too. He once told us of how he aspired to go to Africa to help those in need, to assist those less fortunate than us, as that is what God would want us to do. He wanted to go to seminary school to become a preacher. His religious beliefs were very strong, and he was very vocal about them too, often educating us about them.

For years after the suicide, his words kept ringing in my head. "Suicide is forbidden. Taking one's own life leads them to hell."

My son and I always debated about religion. Though I have been raised a Baptist, I have always been the kind of person that needs to see something in order to believe it. My son, on the other hand, was very strong-minded on faith. We spoke about everything from the Bible, along with faith and religion in general. He was very educated on many different religious beliefs as well, and you could tell he had spent time studying the different aspects of religion. When the topic of suicide was discussed in a religious context, I told him that I thought suicide was a cardinal sin. Our son, apparently, had the same beliefs.

If he was such a strong believer of that, what made him do what he did? What drove him to discard what he so thoroughly believed? What made a religious man risk hell?

Months later, my wife said that she should have paid more attention to his eyes. She said she had noticed that his eyes were lifeless, sparkless and flat during the months leading up to the suicide.

Your eyes are the windows to your soul, they say. And my wife recalls seeing no light in my son's eyes.

Chapter 3: Searching for Answers

"I love you, Mom."

We found the letter on his pillow, properly folded and delicately placed for us to find it there later.

That was it. That was his suicide note.

It offered no explanations and said no goodbyes.

It brought us no answers, no closure, no peace.

To this day, we do not know why our son committed suicide.

We tried getting in touch with anybody he had been in contact with to figure out what was going through his mind. It wouldn't have brought my son back, but it seemed very important to know.

We talked to his friends, and we talked to his preacher.

His friend, the one our son spent most of his time with, refused to give away much information. He only said that our son was in a dark place. He refused to divulge more information, despite our questioning. Whether he was hiding something or not, it was impossible to tell.

The preacher, on the other hand, told us that he and our son had many long talks and debates on the topic of suicide. The preacher had helped him in whatever capacity he could, but for whatever reason, he never reached out to us.

We had no clue. We were entirely oblivious to what 'dark place' he was in and that he was taking an interest in the topic of suicide. He never expressed anything in front of us and never let us get even the slightest whiff of anything being wrong. He was good at hiding emotions.

I wish he didn't feel like he had to hide from his family.

I wish his preacher or his friend would have reached out to us when they sensed something wrong.

Maybe we could all have prevented it. Maybe we could all have stopped him.

Maybe we could all have saved him.

When the police arrived, they went into his room and conducted a thorough search, as is required. They found a bottle of anti-depressants dated December 2016.

Like I said before, we never used to go snooping around his room, so we had no idea. He went to the local clinic, where he was diagnosed with depression and prescribed anti-depressant medication. Of course, the doctors weren't obligated to tell us because he was an adult.

He had been taking anti-depressants for the past month, without our knowledge.

The bottle was almost full; he had stopped taking the medication almost 2 weeks into it.

We knew this because there was no trace of the medication in his body when the coroner performed the autopsy. Our son was clean; there were no medications, illicit drugs, or alcohol in his system.

For further investigation, we went down to the clinic to inquire as to how and why my son was given the anti-depressants in the first place. I was desperate to find out something; anything. Was he truly depressed? What did he say? Did he talk to the doctor there? I was flailing around in the void, trying to get some insight into what was going on in my boy's mind before he took his life.

The local clinic had no answers for me either, though. A sheet of paper determined his diagnosis, not a doctor. I held the generic questionnaire that they hand out to patients to determine if they are depressed and the severity of depression. I scanned the paper.

- *Have you had trouble sleeping?*
- *Have you been having trouble eating?*
- *Do you have a lot of mood swings?*
- *How are your finances?*
- *How is your current relationship?*
- *Have you ever thought about suicide?*

And the list continued. One generic, basic question after another. Eight questions in total. I wondered how this impersonal form could be enough to diagnose someone with depression.

Each question had a numerical value assigned to it. I can't remember what the exact score was in order to be qualified as depressed, but once you hit the 50% mark, the physician would consider you "depressed" and prescribe anti-depressants.

Based on my son's answers to the questionnaire, the clinic had deemed him severely depressed.

The medication they gave him bore a warning label that stated that the medication might increase suicidal tendencies and severity of symptoms in young adults if not monitored properly and followed up with other rehabilitative activities.

Though my son had only taken the medication for barely two weeks, he ended up committing suicide just a month and a half after that.

We hired an attorney. We were going to sue the clinic for their irresponsible handling of a case of severe depression, even by their own silly questionnaire.

I guarantee you that if we were to be judging people on the basis of that form, almost all of America's population would be labeled depressed.

Considering where we are with science and how far we've come in our knowledge of mental health issues, it is an abomination that a questionnaire like that is being used to diagnose depression in young adults. Are there no other, more accurate, more personal ways to do it? Are a bunch of vague and typical questions sufficient in determining the depression level in teens and young adults who can barely explain themselves? The questionnaire seems to be making a mockery of depression and

suicide; nothing more and nothing less. To think that it is designed, endorsed and distributed by a well-known pharmaceutical company is abhorrent, to say the least. They must have years of experience and research under their belt; they should know better. But I suppose a vague questionnaire that would deem half the population as depressed would work better to sell their anti-depressant drugs. These large pharmaceutical companies are only motivated by profits and do not care about the consequences of their careless attitudes that are literally costing lives.

There was another thing that broke my heart upon learning. After his suicide, we obtained Egor's phone records to try and figure out what happened. We noticed an outgoing call to our local family clinic on December 28th. Once we saw that call go out to them, our attorney helped us obtain his medical records.

The medical records show that when he was prescribed the death medication, the doctor informed our son to call her anytime, regardless of the time of the day or night, if he experienced any negative effects of the medication (this comment is documented in hand, corroborated by my son's medical records).

When we called the local clinic concerning the phone call that our son made to them on December 28th, the receptionist said they informed our son that he could not speak to the doctor directly and that he would have to schedule an appointment. The receptionist informed us that doctors do not take personal calls from patients; thus, the message was never forwarded to the doctor. It turned into a small note in their system that a call had come in, and the patient was directed to make an appointment. The next available appointment was on January 17th.

Maybe if he would have scheduled the appointment and went in, everything would be different, and he would be alive today. Maybe if he would have made that appointment, the doctor could have helped him. But that's just my imagination running away with me, creating scenarios that are never going to happen.

I think he felt let down and lied to by the medical field because his doctor told him to call them directly if there were any adverse side effects, but when he finally mustered the courage to call for help, none was provided. In fact, he was dismissed and disregarded, and no concern and assistance extended to him. To an already disturbed young person, that must have been devastating.

Nobody speaks up until something directly affects them. For years, I hadn't given two thoughts about mental health, people's attitude towards it, and how it is being handled in our country. Now, I don't have the luxury of ignorance.

My son was gone, but I could not let the clinic ruin more lives with their irresponsible and careless attitude towards such a serious illness. Depression isn't diagnosed with a form; to be considered depressed, there has to be an in-depth evaluation of each patient. Every patient exhibits different symptoms and signs, which could only be recognized, evaluated and diagnosed by a mental health expert. A more personal method of diagnosis must be utilized prior to putting someone on powerful, mind-altering medication. That is criminal negligence, and I wanted to make the clinic pay for it.

It could not bring my son back; I knew that very well. But it could make someone else's son stay. I didn't want anyone to go through the anguish I went through.

Chapter 4: Life without My Son

Suicide.

We are all aware of the word.

From a 6-year-old child to a 60-year-old adult, we know what suicide means. We've heard it from other distant relatives, old neighbors, and friends of friends. We have seen the news headlines of celebrities committing suicide. We have read stories of great authors and artists putting their heads in the ovens and eating yellow paint because they were too depressed.

Before 2017, suicide was just a word to me. A word that held no real meaning.

Today, it is my reality.

My understanding of the word has changed drastically.

What I have come to realize (or so what my mind and heart tell me to make me feel more at ease) is that suicide is not a cardinal sin at all. I don't know what my son was going through for him to take such a step, but I'm sure that God understands whatever his reasons were. If he was so severely depressed that he saw no way out but suicide, I know God will be considerate. He loves us, after all; he wouldn't punish us for trying to end our suffering, would he? I'm sure my son is safe now, cocooned in a safe corner where he is free from pain. I truly feel that our son is standing next to God and that God has a higher purpose for him.

I also used to think that suicide was due to someone's own weakness. Our son's suicide has changed that perspective completely. Suicide is not for the weak-hearted; it takes a VERY STRONG person to end their life. I know because I have thought about it multiple times in the years after our son passed. I won't lie; I have considered it at least once a week, every week over the last 4 years, but I am way too weak of a man to end my life. I can pick up a gun, but I just can't bring myself to pull the trigger. I have thought of every possible way to end my life, to end my misery, to join my son again on the other side, but I just don't have the nerve to do it. I always chicken out. The fear is more powerful than my anguish.

Our son was a very intelligent, handsome, religious, soft-spoken, and strong young man. We have spoken to several psychologists, and though they all try to give us some relief and comfort, we know we have to find our own closure.

But closure doesn't come easy when you lose someone the way we lost our son. Our lives are not what they were. They never will be without my son. Every time we hear a noise in our home, we question whether it's our son trying to get our attention or trying to communicate with us.

We still can't seem to come to terms with the word suicide. We still can't talk about it openly at home. We change the TV channel every time we hear the word suicide or glimpse a scene where someone is hung or has a rope around their neck. We don't celebrate holidays or birthdays like we used to. Family traditions are no longer an event in our home. Feeling any sort of joy still feels like a task.

There isn't a day that goes by that someone in our family doesn't break down in tears. Four years later, our son's presence and absence are still very powerfully felt. Life will never be the same again. Maybe, we don't want it to be.

We will always keep searching for the true answers. Maybe when we pass away and see him again, the truth will be offered to us. Until then, we must continue living under a dark cloud and wait for the day we reunite with Egor and get our answers.

Nothing is the same without him.

The coroner later informed us that there is a new wave of suicides around, especially through hanging. Maybe he meant to reassure us that we are not alone in our pain and that Egor wasn't the only one who decided to go this way.

Some people find comfort in numbers. If other people have gone through the same, they don't feel singled out for the cruelty, disease, or suffering that they are suffering through. It assures them that their fate was not due to their own deeds and misgivings. It assures them that there are people who share their pain and understand what they are going through.

Let me tell you – when it comes to losing your child, nothing in the world gives you any comfort.

The coroner also painted a more graphic picture of the suicide and reconstructed the entire scene for us, whether we wanted to hear more about it or not. Our son stacked 4 tires on top of each other and balanced himself on top of those tires. He then wrapped the orange strap around his neck and the rafters of the garage ceiling. After that, he simply leaned forward, still standing on the tires. What this does is cut off your circulation, so it's almost as if you simply fall asleep and don't wake up.

This is a far easier approach to suicide because there is no chance of failure and no pain at all. Years ago, victims would stand on a base, and after tying the noose, they would step off the base they were standing on. This method worked most of the time but was painful and always a struggle. The end moments of such suicides must have been excruciating as the person is hit with the realization that they are dying. On the off chance that it wasn't successful, you would have some explaining to do as to why you have a burn mark around your neck.

The image of my son looking into my eyes the moment I opened that side garage door will be etched into my memory for the rest of my life. That image haunts me daily and will for eternity. There is no escaping it. It was difficult to hear the coroner detailing the suicide in-depth, but as strange as it sounds, it also brought me a tiny morsel of fleeting relief. At least Egor wasn't in physical pain in his final moments. He just went to sleep forever.

I didn't have much to hold onto, so I held onto this.

Egor went peacefully and painlessly.

Chapter 5: To the Child Left Behind

We waited until school let out.

At about 2:00 p.m. the same day, I drove over to our daughter's elementary school to pick her up. I always picked her up myself and never let her take the bus.

I was numb, from the top of my head to the bottom of my feet, only focusing on the tasks at hand.

Green light, drive. Red light, Stop

I waited in the parking lot, waiting for them to bring my daughter out.

I couldn't feel a thing. After all the emotions I had felt since the morning, I was empty. Even grief failed me.

I watched the other kids run around, cheerfully and carelessly. It wasn't so long ago when Egor was this small, and I used to pick him up from school.

I wondered if my daughter would ever be this young and careless after today. She will age by years with what she will find out today.

I tried to keep myself composed for my daughter's sake, but the tears streamed down nonetheless.

My daughter appeared, waving to me from afar. As she got into the truck, I greeted her as cheerfully as I could. I knew she could see that I had been crying.

I didn't say a word about what had happened; sitting in a truck without her mommy wasn't the way a 10-year-old girl should find out about her brother's suicide.

I did warn her, though. There was a difficult conversation coming.

"We have some news for you, honey."

I didn't specify whether it was good news or bad, and she didn't ask. Though she was only 10 years old, I knew she had picked up on the mood and had an idea that this probably wasn't going to be the most pleasant of news.

I had hoped that they would be gone by now, but the fire trucks and ambulance were still there when we got home; my son's body was still lying on the ground. A cold body on the cold floor.

I took my daughter straight inside the house, not giving her a chance to look at the horrific scene outside. I didn't want her to see her brother that way. She was too young; the sight would have traumatized her.

I still had no idea how we were going to break the news to her. I had barely processed it myself.

She went up to her room to drop off her backpack while my wife and I braced ourselves for what was coming. Did my young daughter even understand the concept of death fully yet? Did she know what the word 'suicide' meant? Her small, curious brain would have a barrage of questions ready. Could I answer them all?

I guess it didn't matter. As much as I wanted to protect her, I knew we had to find a way to tell her what happened. She was oblivious right now to the hell that had broken loose on our happy home that morning, stomping around the kitchen looking for something to eat, calling out for her mom.

My heart ached for my son, who had felt there was no other way but to take his life, and for my daughter, who had to live with that knowledge now.

She came downstairs and joined us on the couch, her eyes searching ours for an answer.

I glanced at the cupcakes sitting on the kitchen counter. Just last night, Egor and his sister had baked them together and decorated them according to her whims. The cupcakes had barely been eaten yet and looked more like colorful showpieces to brighten up the kitchen.

They had never done that before. I guess it was Egor's last attempt to spend quality time with his sister and to give her something to remember him by.

"We have some bad news. Unfortunately, your brother met with an accident last night and passed away."

We blurted it out, sugarcoating the words, alleviating the impact. Neither my wife or I could utter the word suicide just yet.

But I knew we had to. This wasn't information we should keep from his sister. So eventually, we did tell her that her brother has committed suicide.

She was hysterical. She cried and screamed, grieving the loss she barely even understood yet. We tried to comfort her with hollow words.

He's in a better place now.

His suffering has ended.

He loved you very much.

But she was inconsolable.

She went up to her room afterward and shut the door. For a while, we could hear her sobbing and sniffling, but eventually, a loud silence descended over the house.

There was nothing left to say to each other, and all of us retreated within our own individual grief.

My daughter was completely homeschooled after the incident. Kids can be innocuously judgmental, and after the tragedy, my daughter was branded as the girl whose brother committed suicide. The few friends that she had who supported her through the tough time were gone too.

I wouldn't blame little kids for it. That's the stigma and perception around suicide that society has built, and the kids are simply learning from their environments. Other kids her age possibly did not understand much of suicide either except what they had been told by their parents.

My daughter is 14 years old now, completely isolated with no friends, no social life.

The same could be said about us, to be fair. Though we regularly interact with people due to our home-based business, we do not have any friends. Most people around us do not know how to be our friend, and how to connect to us. I don't blame them either.

Chapter 6: Broken Merchandise

A lot has been written about the pain of losing a child, but experiencing it firsthand was the first time I ever fully understood it.

My wife and I are damaged goods.

Broken merchandise.

Devastated parents.

There was nothing in our lives that was left unaffected by Egor's suicide. To say that our marriage did not suffer as a consequence would be unjust.

Marriages are already complicated enough, but once something like losing a child to suicide is thrown in the mix, it is safe to say that the relationship becomes doomed. Even those who weather through it never really regain the former spark again.

Statistics tell you that 16% of couples divorce after losing a child. I would be lying if I say we never considered or talked about separating. Many a time, we thought both of us would be better off by being away from each other, but it never really happened. As tough as things got between us in the coming months and years, we knew one thing with absolute surety: we love each other dearly.

In fact, I wouldn't be exaggerating it if I said that there was more emotional intimacy after the tragedy. We were, in a way, intertwined because of what we collectively had to go through. The pain connected us to one another, bound us to each other like the strongest glue. We understood what each of us was going through better than anybody else in the whole world. We could have separated and gone our own ways, but I do not believe that either of us could have found someone who would have understood us the way we understood each other. We might have gotten different partners that we could share our joys with, but never one that we could truly share our grief with. My wife and I are broken pieces and only the two of us can ever make sense of it. We are connected through suicide, and we hope to die together.

To say that we were stuck in this marriage because of our daughter would be unfair. We never separated because we didn't want to separate. A lot of things in our relationship never went back to the way they were, but I love my wife, of that I'm sure. We have a relationship unlike that of many others, and we don't expect anybody to understand it, except those who have been through the same as us. Those who have lost their young, beloved child to suicide.

There are so many ways in which our marriage has changed; a lot of it may be what we haven't even recognized yet, while a lot of it is what we have learned to live with. One of the things that strikes me the most is our lack of intimacy.

Perhaps the first big change in our relationship after the death of Egor was the absence of intimacy. We completely and entirely stopped having sex. It has been four years since the tragedy now, but we still cannot be intimate with each other. We have gotten so used to it that it does not even feel strange anymore. What I have learned is that lack of intimacy is not synonymous with lack of love. We love each other infinitely and maybe someday, when the pain subsides, we would be able to discover pleasure in each other again, but until then, this is our life.

Of course, when you're dealing with trauma so enormous, intimacy is the farthest thing from your mind. It has been 4 years, but the pain is still fresh. I think it will always feel fresh. Every day we go to sleep at night and wake up in the morning, the first thing we think about is our son so there is not much else on our minds. It might sound bizarre to everybody, but it doesn't really bother us. The lack of intimacy between us now is just something that is...there. Something that crept into our relationship so naturally that we don't even question its existence anymore. It doesn't feel strange and it doesn't bother us.

Now that I think about it, I might know why we never attempted to address this issue. We've never really talked about it openly, but I'm sure my wife feels the same way I do. Being intimate just feels weird now because we feel that our son might be watching. I know that might sound bizarre, but the thought always crosses my mind and it serves as another reason why we could never even try after 4 years of Egor's death.

No matter how unbearable my own grief seems to me, I am always cognizant of the fact that it must be ten times harder for my wife. He was a son to both of us, but he came out of her womb.

She felt him grow in her womb for months, protecting him from the outside world. She nurtured him for years, taught him everything he knew in life, only for the world outside to tear him down and push him to take his own life.

The child that she had loved way before I even met him had committed suicide. That's another level of trauma that even I can't possibly fathom. I admire her resilience to go on after something like this, and every day I love her even more for it.

We might not have the physical intimacy anymore, but we certainly do have the emotional one. We talk often, and we help each other get through this. We survive, taking one day at a time, pretending to be a normal family. I see the burden that she is carrying, and she can see that I do the same.

Sometimes, we argue over the silliest, most trivial of things but we recognize where it is coming from; so much pent-up grief, and anger, and frustration. We extend the benefit of doubt, and kindness to each other, and we survive.

Chapter 7: Leaving Behind Past Trauma

I know Egor wouldn't have wanted to see his family suffering so much for so long. For his sake, and for our daughter's, I knew we had to get better. We had to get help.

I was astonished to find that in a big city like Spokane, there were absolutely no support groups, or established parties to help bereaved families who have lost a child. In the absence of such support, we did the best we could have. We reached out to churches, and we reached out to online communities on the Internet. We got a lot of love through both, but in reality, it helped us just a little.

Egor was religious, but we never were. We believed in God, yes. But we were not regular churchgoers, and we relied on ourselves more than we relied on God. We tried going to church a few times, but as soon as the preacher started the sermon, I wanted to get up and leave because none of it related to me, none of it connected to my soul. They were mere words, and though that might help some people, it gave me no hope.

There was only one thing that truly did help us, and the only resource we had for any kind of relief and answers. I'm honestly grateful that we found the Hospice of Spokane. The hospice is a non-profit organization that takes care of the family members while an individual is sick or in the end stage of life. They prepare people for what's coming. We discovered one program run by them specifically for families affected by suicide. Everybody there had either lost a child or a spouse to suicide. They were the only people who could understand us.

We went to these 3-hour long meetings every day for the next six months, and it was genuinely the only thing that helped us cope with our reality. Listening to people who had been through a similar ordeal and talking to them knowing that they understood better than most. All of us shared our stories, shared pieces of advice, and shared grief. They listened to us and prepared us for the ocean of emotions that we were feeling and what was coming next. They were our only beacon of hope in a dark, hopeless time, and it made us feel a little less lonely in our despair. Not only did they help us heal from our past traumas, but also gave us hope for the future.

Chapter 8: Moving On and Out

We have bought a new house.

We're finally moving out, just as Egor's 4th death anniversary approaches.

We are moving to a completely different state, to a completely different climate, and to a completely different environment.

We have never been to this state. We haven't even seen the house in person, never walked down its corridors, or gone through the rooms. Of course, we had a video tour but we made the decision without needing much more.

We just want to be out of this house as soon as possible now. This home of ours has housed much more than us; it houses triggers hidden around every corner, it houses resentments in every crevice, it holds grief in every nook, and helplessness in every cranny. This house may have housed my beautiful son too, but it also houses the horrific memories of his suicide.

Maybe a change of place would do us good.

Everything went smoothly. The realtor was great, the transactions were easy, the house is wonderful, the neighborhood is amazing.

We are leaving Washington state, but I sometimes think we are skipping across an entire state just to rid ourselves of the memory of the terrible thing that happened to us here. We are moving in the hopes that being away from this house, this neighborhood, this city, and this state will somehow bring some closure or relief. Even if helps in the tiniest bit, it'll be worth it.

We hope to start our lives afresh, not forgetting the memory of Egor, but to be free of the shackles of grief that his death had placed on us.

There is a difference between being alive and living.

We remind ourselves that we are alive, and we hope to start afresh.

X -x -xx- x-

It's coming up to 4 years since we lost our son. The loss of our son financially destroyed us for a couple of years because our business was established to help others and after the suicide of our son, our minds and hearts went numb. How can you help someone else when you can't even help yourself? We had lost all desire to interact with the world. We were like zombies sifting through the dark. I always ask myself; will our daughter do the same thing?Will I wake up one morning to find that my wife has ended her life?

These questions will continue to trouble me for the rest of my life. But now, there is this tiny flicker of hope. We have decided to take charge of our lives. We have purchased a home in another state where Egor has never been to. We are hopeful that this will be, if not the answer, then a small stepping

stone. Maybe it will help lift the black clouds from over our heads. A new beginning in a new city, and a new home. We might not be there yet, but we are definitely on our way to healing.

The only thought that gives my mind some peace is that there was a bigger purpose for our son, and that God chose him to help others. I have never been a religious man but considering the idea that our son is now doing God's work, and that he is helping others through us gives me a sense of pride and some peace of mind. We have seen and heardthat most families split up or get a divorce after the loss of their child, but thankfully that has not been the case with us. I think what has helped my relationship with my wife is patience and careful choices of words during conversations. My heart and soul are shattered, but my pain could never be close to the pain my wife feels constantly because our son left the last note for her. So, I do my best to be sympathetic, understanding, and patient. I try to be someone that she can lean on.

Together as a family, we are excited about our move. It will be a 180-degree shift in our lives. We

anticipate many days of sunshine; that ever-hanging black cloud will start to turn grey and dissipate soon. One day, the sunlight will penetrate our lives and soak us in its heavenly glow. That day we will rejoice.

We are looking forward to celebrating the holidays again. We hope to become a stronger family after this calamity. The pain and questions will never go away, but we plan on making the best of each day. We are prepared to deal with any problem that arises and we are ready to face the challenges. If we were strong enough to live through the tragic loss of our son, then we can surely deal with the problems that life may throw our way.

We live day by day because tomorrow, life could change. Our son taught us that. We now have a newfound appreciation for our family. We know that our days on this earth are numbered. Our actions, thoughts, and behavior reflect this new perspective on life. We cherish each other's company and appreciate even the smallest of happiness that comes our way.

We are hoping that by leaving everything behind, we can finally breathe, grow, heal, and move on with our lives. That we can carry the memory of Egor and let it be our guiding light as we step into a future of new possibilities.

Chapter 9: A New Beginning

New Year, New Me! Isn't this what they say on New Year's Eve before making New Year's resolutions? But our slogan for the New Year was a little different. As a family, we decided that our slogan for New Year 2021 will be "New Year, New Beginning"!

We left a life behind in Spokane, Washington. A life that was now 1800 miles away from us. As we drove deeper into the State of Iowa, towards our new home, the past traumas, the fears, those loud noises, and everything that had once shaken us awake from our slumber were left far, far behind. Although it was hard to see it, as we all tried to stay calm and look forward to a new beginning, I know that the whole way through, we were letting go of everything, with one deep breath at a time. Every time we exhaled, we broke one link of the chain that had held us back for the past 4 years. We were relieved! For the first time in those tormenting 4 years, we were finally relieved, and we knew that somewhere up there, our son was blessing us on every step of our journey.

As our car stopped in front of our new home, we looked at the majestic Victorian beauty that stood in front of us. Remarkable! The house was nothing short of remarkable! Its large welcoming front door that opens into a sunlit living room and through a narrow corridor takes us right down into our warm, cozy kitchen was the first thing that we noticed.

My daughter jumped right out of the car at the sight of her new home. A home that had been waiting to welcome us in its humble abode. We had made the move with only a few luggage bags in which we had carried our essentials and valuables. The rest of our belongings were to be delivered to us after 2 days via a professional house moving service. We decided to make most of the empty house and got down to planning. We were making mental notes of where we should place our furniture and the rest of the houseware.

Naviira, our cat, looked around the house and gave us his approval in a series of purrs as he walked

elegantly from room to room, impressed with the cheery wood interior of the house. That day, we all had a renewed sense of hope. We were all smiling, planning, and looking forward to a new beginning, in a new home, in a new state, and on this New Year.

We promised ourselves that we would let 2021 be a great year for our family.

I have always been a very practical and rational person. I do believe in God, but I am not the sort of person who believes in hearsay. I look for concrete facts and statistics before agreeing or disagreeing with something.

I have always seen science and faith as two sides of the same coin. Science and faith both help us discover, unfold, and understand the mysteries of the universe. Two paths, that lead to one destination. Whether you use your mind and decide to take the road of intellect to unlock the mysteries of the universe or whether you let your heart and soul guide you as you make your way down the spiritual path, both will lead you to the same destination – an enlightened world.

Earlier, I never found the need to reflect, observe, question, and search the universe for signs. But when Egor left us for another world, a better world, something from deep within me begged me to think, look around and seek for signs. Initially, it was hard to answer that calling. I would be disturbed, sleepless and restless, but I would not know the reason. I knew something inside me was brewing, a feeling of intense desperation, a quest, a thirst, but I did not know how to quench it. The more I ignored it, the stronger it grew until one day, I finally managed to find the oasis my mind, body, and soul had been searching for.

It was the intense need to communicate with my son. To feel his presence around me, and I am very proud to say that I would not have been able to discover it if it wasn't for my wife. She taught me to watch out for signs. She told me that these signs are all around us. The departed souls use the universe as a channel to communicate with the living. Every day they send us signs to let us know that they are here, that they are watching, and they will look out for us.

Since the day I let my guard down, relaxed my mind, and made my body buoyant to flow willingly with the current, I have been becoming increasingly aware of the signs that Egor has been sending us. Unexplainable events that our minds cannot comprehend or explain. But these mysterious signs have helped us in the past and will continue to help my family and me day by day as we move forward in our lives.

It is February 9th, 2021. I am sitting in my favorite recliner, and my wife is close to me on the sofa (an arm's length away), and Naviira is sitting across from me, perched high up on his cat tree, next to a side window where he watches the cars and nature go by.

It is around 7:00 a.m., and we are enjoying a morning cup of coffee in our new home that still amazes us daily with its vintage beauty, elegance, warmth, and homey feeling. My wife are I are talking about our home, the things that we love about it, and how amazing it is that there is absolutely nothing about this house that disappoints us or that we do not enjoy. We are deeply engrossed in conversation, counting the blessings of this treasure that has been presented to our family, and suddenly, a thought occurs to me.

I look at my wife and tell her that lately, I haven't received any sign from our son. Not a single dream, not a single unexplained event, nothing out of the ordinary which should be considered a sign from him. With a heavy heart, I tell my wife that I have been asking for a sign from him to let us know if he approves of our new home and community. But it's already been a couple of days, and I haven't received any sign from him.

Just at that moment, Naviira perks up and starts chattering like there is a squirrel or rabbit outside the window. He starts going crazy with excitement. I walk over to the window to see what all the commotion is about, and to my utter surprise, there is a red robin. The bright crimson robin is sitting on the branch of a tree that is just outside our window. Its feathers were as red as a shiny ruby. I tell my wife what I had just seen and decide to walk back to my recliner. I have seen red robins quite a few times in my 50 years of existence, so I did not think of it as something unusual or out of the ordinary. But my wife darts to the bedroom and comes back with her camera. She urges me to take a picture quickly.

I become puzzled at her suggestion but decide to take a picture anyways. I think that maybe it is because she has never seen a red robin in real life. She knew what a red robin was thanks to all the books she reads and the movies she watches, but this was the first time that she had set her eyes on a real-life red robin.

But later, she explains to me the real reason for her excitement. She informs me that when you see a red robin in its natural surroundings, it is a sign from a departed loved one.

"In truth, one of the most well-known robin symbolic meanings is its connection to death and the afterlife. In general, birds have an ambiguous symbolic significance across cultures and are often thought to bear the spirits of our deceased loved ones. In particular, many red robin superstitions and personal testimonies suggest that robins appear when loved ones are near".

(Source: Gravestones)

That day, my wife had tears streaming down her cheeks for half a day. In her heart, she knew that this was a sign from our son, who had approved of our new home and location. She knew that in the form of a red robin, he had blessed our new home and was just as happy about the move as we were. That night, my wife and I slept well. We knew that a new chapter in our life had begun because our son had helped us turn over the page.

X -x -xx- x- X

A new home, a new state, and a new beginning are proving to be very healthy for our daughter. She has emerges from her room more often and engages in conversations. Sometimes, she even initiates the conversations. She smiles, laughs, chatters with us, and tells us all about her day.

Seeing her coming out of her shell makes me confident that moving into this house was the most powerful thing that we could have done to heal our family.

She is still undecided about what she wants to be when she grows up, but for now, we let her enjoy a carefree life. And every day, we can see her become a little warmer and happier than before.

My daughter was forced to grow up too fast. I know that she feels as if she were robbed of a part of her childhood. At the young age of 10, she had to become an adult and deal with the challenges that none of us were prepared for. Her days of innocence had been turned into the darkest days of her life, and as my wife and I struggled to bounce back from our grief and loss, our daughter silently dealt with the world outside.

She became our strength, our hope, and our reason to continue. In her, we saw a warrior who was not going to let her circumstances get the better of her. She taught us what it was to rise again from the ashes, just like a phoenix, stronger and braver than before. And for that, I will forever be grateful to her.

Her smile, her happiness, and her positive outlook on life give me hope that slowly but surely our family is healing.

As her father, I still watch my daughter's eyes and actions intently. I look for the signs that our son had shown prior to his suicide. My senses are always on high alert. I know that she will not go down the same path as her brother because she feels that pain and can see that pain in our eyes every day. But that fear in my heart has made me twice as vigilant, and I am always on the lookout. I encourage her

to speak her mind so that we know what she has been thinking and feeling. But most importantly, I teach her to be patient and treat others the way she wants to be treated. I am teaching her the importance of being kind. And I am trying my best to explain to her that life is very short. We never know what tomorrow will bring, so we must make the best of today and live, laugh and love while we can.

Chapter 10: Carrying Forward His Legacy

My wife and I were raised to believe in the Golden Rule, which says that you must treat others the way you want to be treated. But over the years, a series of bad experiences taught us to become a little cautious. We became careful with who we trusted and lent a helping hand to. When we would see homeless people and drug addicts on the road, we would turn our gaze the other way. I always told myself that it is pointless to help them. I used to think that they are in this situation because of their own irresponsible actions. My philosophy was that you cannot help someone if they don't want to be helped. I blamed their misery on their mindset because if you want to change your circumstances, you work for it.

But Egor was different. To him, the cause and after effects didn't matter. All he saw was someone in dire need. Someone who needed his help and maybe was too shy to ask for it. My son taught us that random acts of kindness are always rewarded and reciprocated.

When we would be on the road, and if we happened to pass by a homeless person, he would make me pull over our car. He would roll down the window and give away all the cash that he would be carrying in his wallet to the homeless person. And this was not a one-time thing. He would do this out of habit every time that we passed by someone who seemed to need help. Back then, this habit of his would infuriate me. I never stopped him or voiced my objection, but I did try to explain to him that most probably, the homeless person will use this cash to buy more drugs and alcohol. To be honest, I was afraid that people would take advantage of my son's kind heart and rob him of his hard-earned money. But he did not care for that. To him, all that mattered was that he had done his part in making the world a better place.

He was very generous with his money. Without a second thought, he would empty his wallet when someone was in need of money. I think that's the legacy he left behind. His legacy of performing random acts of kindness.

After he left us, my wife and I decided to carry forward his legacy. We stopped seeing people as victims of their own folly and failings and instead became more empathetic. After our great loss and seeing the reaction of the world to it, where everybody was quick to judge and blame us, we decided that we will never judge a person by their situation. Now we understand. Now we emphasize. Now we follow in our son's footsteps and try to help people in whatever way we can.

When we were finalizing the deal for our new home in Iowa, we found our kindness being reciprocated in so many beautiful ways. We were so pleased with all the people who had helped us through this big move that we decided to offer our thanks a little differently. And I know that Egor played a big part in it.

In December 2020, the sellers of our new house agreed to accept our offer and decided to sell the house to us. I had to send our realtor an earnest money check to go towards closing. In the same envelope, I wrote an additional check for $1000.00 and asked our realtor to give this gift to a family or families in the local community that may be struggling financially and were unable to celebrate a warm and enjoyable Christmas holiday with their loved ones.

We had requested our realtor that he should not tell the family or families where the money came from. We wanted this gift it to be strictly anonymous. Our intention was just to touch some lives with a genuinely nice act of kindness.

We did the same with our home inspector. In December 2020, we had hired an inspection company to inspect our new home. The same home that we had never set foot in prior to moving in it. Once the inspection was complete, I had to mail a check to the owner of the home inspection company to pay for the services he has performed at our new home. Along with the check for his service charges, I included a check for $500.00 and sent him the same instructions that I had sent to the realtor who had helped us with the purchase of our new home. To our surprise, the owner of the inspection company, Greg, not only distributed our $500.00 amongst the needy in his community but also took out $500.00 from his own pocket and distributed it amongst his four children. His children were given the same instructions as I had given to Greg, and even though they had the option to keep a little for themselves

for the holiday season, they gave it all away. Some of the cash was given away as dollar bills, while some of it was spent on buying food and presents for the underprivileged.

So not only did we surprise this home inspector with our random act of kindness, but he doubled our gift and taught his children to perform random acts of kindness in this little town of Iowa.When Greg told me what he had done, I simply fell out of my chair with joy. I knew that Egor had a hand in it and that he was watching it all unfold before his eyes with great pride.

We arrived at our new home on January 9th, 2021, and the home-delivered 1000 times more than what we could have ever imagined. It was hard to believe that we had purchased this haven while we were 1800 miles away from it. We had never physically stepped foot inside this house prior to purchasing it. But this house surprised us by being a lot more than what we had expected it to be. In fact, sometimes, we think like we don't deserve a house as elegant and as beautiful as this.

To help us move our belongings from Washington to Iowa, we hired the services of a moving company. The moving company arrived 4 days after we did. There were two full-sized semi-trailers that were loaded with our stuff.

A young man by the name of Jake brought his two-men crew to our home to unload the trailers and place the items in our new home. Jake is the same age as our son and shockingly similar in appearance. The way he was dressed, his entire attitude and demeanor reminded my wife and me of our son. As we looked at this young man, working so hard to help us settle in our new home, we kept thinking about our firstborn. It felt as if it was Egor, standing before our eyes, unloading the furniture and houseware in our new home. From time to time, my wife and I shed tears and silently felt grateful for Jake's presence.

Once Jake and his crew were done with the work and had left, I sent him a text message asking him for his PayPal email address. The following day, I sent Jake a friend-to-friend donation of $1000.00 and could not thank him enough for coming by our home and being a part of our family for the day. After a few hours, I went up to my wife and told her what I had done. She smiled and started tearing up again. What she said next left me completely surprised. She informed me that she had handed Jake $500.00 in cash while he was finishing up with the unloading of our items. She would have given more, but that was all the cash she had in her purse. I had no idea she did this. But I was really happy to hear of it. Jake is an extremely hard worker and a thoughtful young man. Unfortunately, the median income here in Iowa is lower than the national average. People find it challenging to make their ends meet. We know that Jake deserves so much more, and we felt truly blessed that we were given the opportunity to help this young man.

7 months after our son's suicide, we had heard that there was going to be a solar eclipse in Seattle, Washington. This was going to be a rare occasion. But my family and I will remember August 17th, 2017, for an entirely different reason.

My wife and I thought that this solar eclipse would help us get our daughter out of the house and

experience something wonderful for a change. We traveled to Seattle and booked a hotel for the weekend. In Seattle, one of our favorite places to explore is Pike's Place Market. There are so many shops and things to look at. We decided to walk down 7 blocks to the market. On our way, we saw two homeless people sitting on a bench at a bus stop. It is my guess, and I may be wrong, but they looked like a couple. They did not say anything or even looked at us, but my wife told me to wait for a minute. She opened her purse and took out some cash. She handed the money to these two strangers. They thanked us, and we moved on.

After looking around the Pike's Place Market, we headed back to the hotel because it was almost time for the solar eclipse. I could see my daughter's excitement in her quick steps and her gleeful smile. When we were near our hotel, the three of us found a small spot on the corner of the street. People were already gathered here to witness this rare event. We were really happy to have found the best view. But our excitement was short-lived. We noticed that everyone was wearing special glasses. I asked a man who was standing nearby for some clarification. He said that viewing the sun directly can be very harmful for the eyes. That's why you need solar viewers, an eyewear designed specially to view the sun, to witness the solar eclipse. You should have seen the instant disappointment on our daughter's face. It was the same feeling of disappointment that athletes feel when they are so close to winning the race but stumble and fall down just one foot away from the finish line.

My wife told me to stay with our daughter and save our spot on the sidewalk while she went down to the market to purchase the solar viewers. The sight that I witnessed next was more rare to me than the solar eclipse ever will be. She sprinted all the way down to the market to make sure that she made it back in time with solar viewers to help her daughter see the solar eclipse. Let me tell you, folks, neither my wife nor I enjoy jogging or running. We live a sedentary life, mostly because our work commitments keep us home-bound. But to see her sprint down the market in search of solar viewers is a sight I will never forget.

She returned 15 minutes later with tears running down her face. When I asked her the reason, she explained that when she went inside the store, the clerk informed her that all the solar viewers had been sold out. My wife knew that it would shatter our daughter's heart. She was so excited about the event, and we had come all the way for it. To leave Seattle without witnessing the solar eclipse would have broken her heart. Our little angel had already been through so much within these past few months.

My wife was finding the right words to break the news to our daughter. But just then, a man reached out to my wife and handed her three pairs of solar eclipse viewing glasses. Exactly three! He did not say a single word. He just handed the glasses to my wife and vanished as silently as he came. To this date, I still wonder about that man. How did he know that there were three of us? How did he know that my wife was searching for solar viewers, and who was this guy? But something in my heart tells me that our son, our beloved Egor played an instrumental role in making this day one of the most special days we could have hoped for. He was the kind of big brother who always looked out for his little sister. Maybe this was his way of telling us that he will always watch over his baby sister.

Whatever it may have been, one thing is certain, we performed a random act of kindness that day by helping that homeless couple at the bus stop, and we saw the kindness being reciprocated in the guise of that stranger who handed my wife three solar viewers.

After that day, as a family, we have decided to stay true to his legacy, and now, whenever we get the

chance, we try to help people to the best of our abilities because we know that if our son was here, he would have surely done that.

Chapter 11: The Message

In these 4 years, every single person that I shared my sorrow with told me just one thing...time is the greatest healer. They told me to give it some time because slowly life goes back to normal and you learn to smile again.

I have been through days when just opening my eyes in the morning seemed like a struggle. I didn't want to wake up. I didn't want to face another day. I would beg for God to end it all. With closed eyes I would pray to him saying "God! Please let it all just be a hellish nightmare." And even though something in my mind would tell me that it was absurd to have that hope, I would still hope that when I will open my eyes our lives would be just like they were before that fateful morning.

The funny thing about time is that it never stops. Even if you sit completely still, do nothing, think nothing, and even feel nothing, the world around you keeps moving. I guess this is what happened with the three of us. The earlier days felt like we were in a trance. We were seeing everything but not really believing it. We were hearing everything, but not really listening to it. It felt as if we were neither living nor dead. But we survived. And one day, we finally snapped out of the trance and reminded ourselves that life must go on. We accepted the reality, acknowledged the pain and emptiness but decided that even though nothing will ever be the same, we must open our hearts to good things in life.

It is said that the universe aligns itself to your energy and vibration. It returns to you what you put into it. When your aura reeks of hate, anger and pessimism, you receive the same things in return. But when you cleanse your soul, become a better version of yourself and raise your vibration, the universe offers you the best things in life. We live by this guiding principle now.

And this is why I would like to end my book with a message of hope.

To the Young Adults Who Are Going Through a Tough Time:

My children, it may seem like you are living a life that is meaningless and nobody in this world understands you but trust me, you will always find people who do. You have to reach out to people and talk to them. Everybody in this world goes through their own struggles. Nobody has it easy. But what really matters is how you deal with it.

The minute you start talking to people and hearing their stories, you will realize that nothing in this world is permanent, not even hardships, pain and despair. Life is a great leveler. It gives you both, the good and the bad. It really depends on what you acknowledge and focus on. Just for a minute, close your eyes and think of all the blessings that you have today- parents, friends, a roof over your head, food on the table, and a body that was created with perfection to make a difference in the world. But instead, what most of us focus on are the things that we don't have.

If we just change our question from "Why don't I have it?" to "Why do I have it", our lives will change for the better. We will begin to see that everything in our life has a purpose. We met the wrong ones because we had to appreciate the right ones. We lost a few things along the way because we had to unload and unburden ourselves before picking up newer and better things. And we had to fall down and break into pieces so that this time we would have the choice to recreate ourselves the way we

like.

Running away from life does not solve a problem. In fact, its ripple effects will be felt by your loved ones for years. And there is no problem in the world that cannot be solved with honest and open communication. Years from now, you will be laughing about this moment because by then you will have reached such a great height in life that today's problems will look small and insignificant. But if today everything around you seems hopeless and you have nowhere else to turn, just consider my heartfelt advice. Live your life one day at a time. You don't have to run, you don't even have to walk, just crawl and take one small baby step at a time. Focus on the positive and try to make the best of each day. Just make sure that every night, before sleeping you can tell yourself that you gave it your best. Because my child, in the end that's all that matters.

To the Parents Who Have Suffered the Loss of Their Child:

I wish I had a magic wand and could stop this pain for you. It has been a little over 4 years since we lost our son, and the pain and heartache will never go away. I read a quote somewhere which said,

> *"A wife who loses a husband is called a widow.*
>
> *A husband who loses a wife is called a widower.*
>
> *A child who loses his parents is called an orphan.*
>
> *There is no word for a parent who loses a child.*
>
> *That's how awful the loss is."*

As a father who lost his son to suicide, I can tell you that no amount of happiness can ever fill that void that you feel in your heart. I can understand that in this moment you believe that you will never be happy. You might even be pushing away the ones who genuinely care about you and are trying so hard to make you smile because you feel like you don't deserve it but trust me, it does get easier as time goes by.

Together, you and your family will go through several stages of grief and I think that you need to go through them in order to heal. Be strong, be patient and be extremely supportive of one another. You have to battle it out as a family. Appreciate the little things they have been doing to cheer you up. Understand that they need you too so instead of pushing them away, share your pain and sorrow with them because maybe these shared emotions will bring you closer and you will develop a bond much stronger than before.

To all the husbands and boyfriends who have lost their child, this will be the defining moment of your relationship with the mother of your lost child. Please, be extremely patient and understanding to your spouse or partner. I assure you that the pain you are feeling today is nowhere comparable to the pain of the mother who has lost their child. She carried her child in her womb for 9 months. With a smile she withstood the bone breaking pain that she felt at the birth of her child and without complaints she spent countless sleepless nights feeding, nurturing and protecting the child that came out of her. Therefore, her connection to her lost child will always be much deeper and stronger than yours. She gave the child her selfless love and devotion and formed an emotional and physical bond so deep that even when the child is not around, she can always feel their presence.

I understand that you feel like you cannot breathe and that the whole world as you knew it has stopped. Now consider the fact that your wife's pain is 10 times worse. So, please be patient, kind and understanding to your wife and be the best supportive partner you can be during this time of hurt and pain.

To Surviving Family Members of Loved Ones Who Committed Suicide:

There is no shame in admitting that after the losing my son, I too developed suicidal tendencies. We have stigmatized depression and suicide and associated it with weakness. But the truth is very different. For a moment just think how much pain a person must be in that they decide to end their lives. It takes a lot of courage to plan and carry out your own death. It's not an impulsive or hasty decision. But when something inside you breaks and you can feel no way out, it may seem like the only option left. Driven by pain, hopelessness and anger, a person may resort to suicide instead of looking for help. So, please don't blame the ones who took their lives because you will never be able to relate to their emotional state. Instead, try to find ways to lessen the stigma around suicide and deteriorating mental health.

In-order to heal from the pain, you must look for other families or loved ones that have lost someone to suicide. These people, such as I, utterly understand what you are feeling and going through. They can rightly predict what you will be feeling and going through tomorrow, next week, next year and throughout your life because you are connected to them through shared experiences, loss and pain.

Over the next couple of years, your day-to-day life will be numb and meaningless. Try your best to find something to hold onto. Try to find new meaning and purpose in your life.

The most important thing I can say is watch for the signs. They will come when you least expect them. Try to believe in the higher power, whether it is religion or the universe. Try to believe that everything happens for a reason and see the bigger picture. Every action leads to another action. Don't judge and be patient with your neighbors or friends when they say, "Sorry for your loss." For years I hated hearing that statement because whoever said that to me had no idea what the loss of a child really felt like. But understand that your friends and neighbors care about you and are truly trying to help you in this difficult time. They just don't know how to act or help so they say what everyone is tuned to say, "Sorry for your Loss."

Hopefully in the future, I will have the nerve to travel around the U.S. and offer meetings to help you heal. Maybe I will even conduct seminars at different high schools to educate our young adults on suicide and the butterfly effect damage of that one single action but for now just remember my words and be kind to yourself.

To the World:

Only light can pierce through darkness. Only courage can tear down walls of fear. Only love can melt hatred and only compassion can eliminate indifference. Just like us, the world needs healing, and yes, it can start with you.

Try and perform one random act of kindness. Simply smile to someone passing by and greet them warmly. You never know, a simple "Good morning!" just be might be what that stranger needs to feel

hopeful again. With your kind words and a beautiful, warm smile you may just change someone's life and encourage them to carry forward the good will.

Everyone has heard of the word suicide and knows its meaning, but for most it is just a word. An action that happens to someone else in the world. This one small, three syllable word...SUICIDE, has no real meaning, until it happens to someone in your family or friend circle. Then, it is not just a word in the dictionary, it is REAL. Take the time to imagine losing a loved one to suicide tomorrow. What would you do differently today if you knew what tomorrow was bringing? Think about it! Hug your family and tell them how much they mean to you because life may never give you another chance.

And lastly, I hope that by reading my story, people who have lost their loved ones to suicide will find some sort of solace. That by understanding the pain that Egor felt in the last days of his life, we will be able to erase the stigma associated with suicide because for every life that is lost this way, society is equally to be blamed. As a father, husband, and survivor, I appeal to the world... Be kind!

CPSIA information can be obtained
at www.ICGtesting.com
Printed in the USA
LVHW060318180222
711411LV00007B/415